CAREER AI: NAVIGATING THE JOB MARKET IN THE AGE OF ARTIFICIAL INTELLIGENCE

Michael R. Watson

This book is dedicated to both of my parents, Devon and Carole Watson. You taught me that it's not how many times you get knocked down that count, it's how many times you get back up! Thank you for your unconditional love.

-Michael

CONTENTS

Title Page
Dedication
Chapter 1: The Rise of AI and Its Impact on the Job Market: 1
Chapter 2: Navigating the Digital Landscape: Online Job Search Strategies   4
Chapter 3: Mastering the Art of Networking in a Digital World   8
Chapter 4: Crafting a Winning Resume and Cover Letter with AI in Mind   12
Chapter 5: Preparing for the AI-Enabled Job Interview: Tips and Techniques   16
Chapter 6: Upgrading Your Skills for the Age of AI: Training and Education   21
Chapter 7: Job Opportunities in Emerging AI Fields   24
Chapter 8: Overcoming the Challenges of Working with AI and Robots   27
Chapter 9: Balancing the Human Touch and AI in Your Career   30
Chapter 10: Staying Ahead of the Curve: Future-Proofing Your Career in the Age of AI   32
Chapter 11: Ethical Considerations for AI-Enabled Careers: Making Responsible Choices   35
Chapter 12: Working with AI in Teams: Collaborating with Machines and Humans   38

Chapter 13: Building Your Personal Brand in the Digital Age: Strategies and Best Practices — 41

Chapter 14: Overcoming Ageism and Bias in the AI-Driven Job Market — 45

Chapter 15: The Future of Work: Anticipating and Adapting to AI-Driven Changes — 48

Chapter 16: The Role of Emotional Intelligence in the Age of AI — 52

Chapter 17: AI and the Gig Economy: Opportunities and Challenges — 55

Chapter 18: Navigating the Global Job Market with AI: Tips and Strategies — 58

Chapter 19: The Intersection of AI and Creativity: Opportunities and Challenges for Creative Careers — 61

Chapter 20: AI and Your Personal Life: Finding Work-Life Balance in the Digital Age — 65

About The Author — 69

CHAPTER 1: THE RISE OF AI AND ITS IMPACT ON THE JOB MARKET:

Artificial intelligence (AI) is a rapidly growing field that is transforming the way we live and work. From self-driving cars to personalized medical treatments, AI is revolutionizing many industries and creating new opportunities for workers. However, the rise of AI is also causing concern about the impact it will have on the job market.

The Impact of AI on Jobs

The impact of AI on jobs is a complex issue that has been the subject of much debate. While some experts predict that AI will lead to widespread job loss, others argue that it will create new jobs and lead to a more efficient and productive workforce. In reality, the impact of AI on jobs is likely to be a combination of both.

According to a report by the McKinsey Global Institute, up to 375 million workers worldwide may need to switch occupational categories by 2030 because of automation. This means that many workers will need to retrain and learn new skills to stay competitive in the job market.

The Jobs Most At Risk of Automation

AI has the ability to automate many routine and repetitive tasks. This means that jobs that involve manual labor, data entry, or other routine tasks are at the highest risk of automation. For example, self-driving trucks may replace truck drivers, and chatbots may replace customer service representatives.

However, jobs that require creativity, problem-solving, and emotional intelligence are less likely to be automated. This includes jobs in fields such as healthcare, education, and the arts, where human interaction and creativity are essential.

The Jobs Created by AI

While some jobs are at risk of automation, AI is also creating new job opportunities in emerging fields such as machine learning, data science, and robotics. These fields require specialized skills and knowledge, and there is a growing demand for workers with these skills.

In addition, as AI is integrated into more industries, there will be an increasing demand for workers with skills in areas such as cybersecurity, privacy, and ethics. These skills will be essential for ensuring that AI is used in a responsible and ethical manner.

Adaptability and Flexibility

One of the key challenges for workers in the age of AI is the need to be adaptable and flexible. As new technologies and industries emerge, workers will need to be able to learn and adapt quickly to new roles and environments. This requires a mindset of lifelong learning and a willingness to embrace new technologies and ways of working.

This adaptability and flexibility will be especially important for workers whose jobs are at risk of automation. Workers in these roles will need to be able to learn new skills and transition to new roles as their industries change.

Government and Business Response to AI

Governments and businesses are also starting to respond to the impact of AI on the job market. Some governments are implementing policies and programs to help workers retrain and acquire new skills. For example, the European Union has created the European Globalization Adjustment Fund to help workers who have lost their jobs due to globalization and technological change.

Businesses are also starting to invest in training and reskilling programs for their employees. In addition, many companies are exploring the use of AI to improve their operations and increase efficiency.

Conclusion

The rise of AI presents both challenges and opportunities for the job market. While some jobs will undoubtedly be automated, new roles and career paths will also be created. The key for job seekers is to stay informed about the impact of AI on their industry, to be proactive about developing new skills, and to embrace a mindset of lifelong learning and adaptability. By doing so, workers can position themselves to take advantage of the opportunities presented by AI and thrive in the jobs of the future.

CHAPTER 2: NAVIGATING THE DIGITAL LANDSCAPE: ONLINE JOB SEARCH STRATEGIES

The digital landscape has fundamentally changed the way we search for jobs. With the rise of online job boards, social media, and networking platforms, job seekers have access to a wealth of information and opportunities. However, navigating this digital landscape can be overwhelming and confusing. In this chapter, we will explore some effective strategies for navigating the online job search process.

Creating an Online Presence

The first step in navigating the digital landscape is to establish a strong online presence. This includes creating a professional profile on LinkedIn and other social media platforms, as well as building a personal website or online portfolio. Your online presence should showcase your skills, experience, and accomplishments and make it easy for potential employers to find you.

Using Online Job Boards

Online job boards such as Indeed, Monster, and Glassdoor are a valuable resource for job seekers. These platforms allow you to search for jobs based on your skills and experience, and provide a wealth of information about job openings, salaries, and company reviews. In addition, many job boards offer tools to help you create a resume or cover letter, and allow you to set up job alerts so that you are notified when new jobs that match your criteria are posted.

Networking on Social Media

Social media platforms such as LinkedIn, Twitter, and Facebook can be powerful tools for networking and building relationships with potential employers. By joining industry-specific groups and participating in online discussions, you can connect with people in your field and stay up to date on industry news and trends. In addition, you can use social media to follow companies you are interested in and to keep an eye on job openings.

Reaching Out to Your Network

While online networking is important, it's also important to reach out to your personal and professional network. Let your friends, family, and colleagues know that you are looking for a job and ask if they know of any openings or can make any introductions. In addition, reach out to former colleagues or managers and ask for recommendations or references. Personal connections can be a valuable asset in the job search process.

Advantages of Being Hired by Referral

One of the advantages of networking and reaching out to your personal and professional network is the potential to be hired by referral. Being referred for a job by someone who knows you and your work can be a powerful advantage in the hiring process. According to a study by Jobvite, referrals are the top source of external hires, accounting for 30% of all hires.

When you are referred for a job, you already have a foot in the door. The person who referred you can vouch for your skills, experience, and work ethic, which can give you a significant advantage over other candidates. In addition, being referred for a job can increase your chances of getting an interview. Many companies have employee referral programs, which give priority to candidates who are referred by current employees.

One last thought on referrals. Many companies have generous Employee Referral Programs that pay employees upwards of $5,000 USD for referring a candidiate that eventually get hired. Take advantage of this and utilize LinkedIn to identify who you know or have common interest with. You don't need to personally know the person. You can ask an alumni of a school you attended or perhaps someone you share common interests with. The bottom line is, get referred in. I'll explain to you why this is so important in the next section.

Applying for Jobs Online

Know this - Your odds of getting a job when applying online are 1 in 200. When referred into a job, your odds are 1 in 10.

Always look to be referred in. With that being said, applying for jobs online is a necessary evil and it's important to customize your application for each job. This means tailoring your resume and cover letter to the specific requirements of the job, and highlighting your relevant experience and skills. In addition, make sure that you follow the application instructions carefully and that your application is free of errors.

Conclusion

Navigating the digital landscape can be a challenging and overwhelming task, but by following these online job search strategies, job seekers can increase their chances of finding the right job. Whether you are using online job boards, networking on social media, or reaching out to your personal network, building a strong online presence and tailoring your applications to each job can help you stand out in a crowded field of candidates. By leveraging the power of technology and making the most of your personal connections, you can navigate the digital landscape with confidence and land your dream job. While being hired by referral may give you a leg up in the hiring process, applying for jobs online is still an important part of the job search process. By combining these strategies and staying focused on your career goals, you can successfully navigate the job market in the age of AI.

CHAPTER 3: MASTERING THE ART OF NETWORKING IN A DIGITAL WORLD

In the digital age, networking has become more important than ever. The rise of social media and other online platforms has made it easier to connect with people in your industry and build relationships with potential employers. However, navigating the world of digital networking can be daunting. In this chapter, we will explore some effective strategies for mastering the art of networking in a digital world.

Building Your Network

Building your network is an ongoing process that requires time and effort. The first step is to identify people you want to connect with. This can include industry leaders, colleagues, alumni from your university, and people you have met at industry events. You can use LinkedIn, Twitter, and other social media platforms to search for people in your industry and to connect with them.

When reaching out to people, it's important to be clear about your intentions and to be respectful of their time. You should also personalize your message and explain why you want to connect with them. It's important to make the connection about them, not just about what they can do for you.

Leveraging Social Media

Social media is a powerful tool for networking, but it's important to use it strategically. LinkedIn is the most popular platform for professional networking, and it's important to have a complete and professional profile. You should include a professional headshot, a summary of your skills and experience, and a list of your achievements. You should also be active on the platform by sharing articles, commenting on other people's posts, and engaging with industry leaders.

Twitter is another platform that can be useful for networking. You can use Twitter to connect with people in your industry, share your work, and engage in online discussions. You should use hashtags to join relevant conversations and to make it easier for people to find your content.

Attending Industry Events

Attending industry events is a great way to build your network and to learn about the latest trends and developments in your field. You should research events in your industry and prioritize the ones that are most relevant to your career goals. Before attending an event, it's important to have a clear goal in mind and to prepare questions and talking points.

When attending an event, you should make an effort to meet new people and to engage in conversations. You should be genuine and interested in what other people have to say. It's important to follow up after the event by sending a thank-you note or connecting on social media.

Engaging with Recruiters

Recruiters can be a valuable resource in your job search, but it's important to approach them strategically. You should research recruiting agencies and recruiters in your industry and identify those who specialize in your field. You should also make sure that your resume and cover letter are well-crafted and targeted to the specific job or industry.

When engaging with recruiters, it's important to be professional and responsive. You should be clear about your career goals and your availability for interviews. You should also be prepared to answer questions about your skills and experience.

Staying in Touch

Staying in touch with people in your network is important for building and maintaining relationships. You should follow up after meetings, send occasional emails or messages, and stay active on social media. It's important to be thoughtful and genuine in your interactions and to add value to your network.

Conclusion

Networking is a critical part of building a successful career in the digital age. By building your network, leveraging social media, attending industry events, engaging with recruiters, and staying in touch with people in your network, you can master the art of networking in a digital world. Whether you are looking for a new job or seeking to advance your career, networking can help you achieve your goals and build a fulfilling and successful career.

8 Quick Tips For For Mastering The Art Of Networking In A Digital World:

1. Be strategic in your networking efforts. Before reaching out to people, do some research to identify those who are most likely to be valuable connections. Think about your career goals and the types of people who can help you achieve them.
2. Personalize your messages. When you reach out to someone, take the time to personalize your message and explain why you want to connect with them. It's

important to make the connection about them, not just about what they can do for you.
3. Join relevant groups and communities. There are many online communities and groups focused on specific industries or career paths. Joining these groups can be a great way to connect with people who share your interests and to learn about job opportunities.
4. Attend virtual events. In addition to in-person industry events, there are many virtual events that you can attend from the comfort of your own home. Look for webinars, conferences, and other online events that are relevant to your career goals.
5. Use social media to share your work. In addition to connecting with people, social media can be a great way to showcase your skills and experience. Share your work on social media platforms like LinkedIn and Twitter, and engage with other people's posts.
6. Be respectful of people's time. When reaching out to someone, be clear about your intentions and be respectful of their time. Don't ask for too much right away, and be willing to take the time to build a relationship before asking for favors.
7. Follow up after meetings and events. After meeting someone at an event or having a conversation with them online, it's important to follow up. Send a thank-you note or message, and try to keep the conversation going.
8. Be genuine and authentic. People can tell when you're not being genuine or authentic, and it can be a turnoff. Be yourself, and be interested in what other people have to say.

By using these strategies and tips, you can build a strong network of professional contacts and increase your chances of landing your dream job in the age of AI.

CHAPTER 4: CRAFTING A WINNING RESUME AND COVER LETTER WITH AI IN MIND

Your resume and cover letter are crucial documents when it comes to landing your dream job, and in the age of AI, it's more important than ever to craft these documents with AI in mind. In this chapter, we will cover the key strategies for creating a resume and cover letter that will not only catch the attention of human recruiters but also be optimized for AI algorithms.

First, it's essential to understand the basics of resume and cover letter writing. Your resume should be easy to read, organized, and highlight your skills and experience in a way that aligns with the job you're applying for. Your cover letter should complement your resume and tell your potential employer why you're the best fit for the job.

However, it's not enough to simply create a visually appealing resume and cover letter. Many companies use AI algorithms to screen applications before they ever reach human recruiters. This means that your resume and cover letter must also be optimized for AI algorithms to ensure they don't get rejected before they reach the hands of a human recruiter.

One way to do this is to make sure that your resume and cover letter contain relevant keywords. These keywords should be specific to the job you're applying for and be included in a way that doesn't look like you're just stuffing your documents with words. By doing this, you increase the chances of your application getting through the initial AI screening.

It's also important to pay attention to the formatting of your documents. While a creative and visually appealing design can help your application stand out, it's essential to remember that the formatting must also be AI-friendly. This means that it should be straightforward, easy to read, and not contain any unique formatting that could cause the AI to reject your application.

Customizing your resume and cover letter to match the specific job requirements is another crucial step in optimizing your application for both human recruiters and AI algorithms. This includes researching the company and the job requirements to make sure that your application is tailored to the specific position you're applying for. It's not enough to just send a generic resume and cover letter to multiple job postings. Customizing your application can help you stand out and show the hiring manager that you've done your research.

While it's essential to craft a winning resume and cover letter with AI in mind, you don't have to do it alone. Many AI-powered tools can help you create a visually appealing and AI-friendly resume and cover letter. These tools can scan job descriptions to find the most relevant keywords and phrases and help you format your documents in a way that's optimized for AI algorithms. It's important to remember that these tools should be used as a supplement to your own creativity and research.

Finally, it's important to remember some general tips for creating a winning resume and cover letter. This includes proofreading your documents, including your contact information, and making sure that your documents are visually appealing and easy to read. Remember that your resume and cover letter are often the first impression that a potential employer has of you, so make sure that they represent you in the best possible light.

The 4 Keys To Crafting A Winning Resume And Cover Letter With Ai In Mind;

1. One of the key ways to ensure that your resume and cover letter are optimized for AI algorithms is to use a standard and simple font. While some creative and unique fonts can look visually appealing, they can also be difficult for AI algorithms to read. This can result in your application being rejected even if it meets all the necessary job requirements. By using a standard font such as Arial or Times New Roman, you can increase the chances of your application making it through the AI screening process.
2. Another strategy for optimizing your resume and cover letter for AI algorithms is to use bullet points instead of paragraphs. This makes your application easier to read and scan for AI algorithms. Additionally, using bullet points helps to break up the text and make your skills and experience stand out to human recruiters.
3. When customizing your resume and cover letter, it's important to focus on the skills and experience that are most relevant to the job you're applying for. While it's tempting to include all of your skills and experience, doing so can make your application seem cluttered and unfocused. Instead, focus on the key skills and experience that align with the job requirements. This can help to ensure that your application stands out to both human recruiters and AI algorithms.
4. Lastly, it's important to proofread your resume and cover letter carefully. Have a friend or family member also read it. Trust me when I tell you, they will catch things you miss. While AI algorithms may not pick up on spelling or grammatical errors, human recruiters will. Any mistakes in your application can make you seem unprofessional and unprepared. Take the time to read through your documents multiple times to catch any errors before submitting your application.

Conclusion

By following these strategies and tips, you can create a winning resume and cover letter that not only catches the attention of human recruiters but is also optimized for AI algorithms. You have one chance at a first impression so don't mess it up by being lazy and not proofreading. These tips will help to increase your chances of getting past the initial screening process and land your dream job in the age of AI.

CHAPTER 5: PREPARING FOR THE AI-ENABLED JOB INTERVIEW: TIPS AND TECHNIQUES

Understanding AI-Enabled Job Interviews:

Definition of AI-enabled job interviews: AI-enabled job interviews use various types of AI technology, such as natural language processing, machine learning, and facial recognition, to conduct job interviews with candidates.

- Types of AI-powered job interviews:

    o Video interviews: These are similar to traditional interviews but conducted remotely using video conferencing tools. The AI technology used may include video analytics to analyze the candidate's facial expressions, tone of voice, and body language.

    o Chatbot interviews: These use a chatbot or virtual assistant to conduct the interview. The AI technology used may include natural language processing to understand the candidate's responses and provide automated follow-up questions.

- o   Predictive analytics interviews: These use algorithms to analyze the candidate's data, such as their resume and social media profiles, to predict their job performance and fit.

- The benefits and drawbacks of AI-enabled job interviews:

  - o   Benefits: AI-enabled job interviews can save time and resources, provide standardized and objective evaluations, and reduce bias in the hiring process.

  - o   Drawbacks: AI technology may not always accurately assess candidates, may be biased or discriminatory, and may limit opportunities for personal connection and rapport-building.

Preparing for an AI-Enabled Job Interview:

- Research the company and job position: Conduct thorough research on the company and job position to understand their values, mission, and culture. This can help you tailor your responses to the interviewer's expectations and demonstrate your fit for the role.

- Practice answering common interview questions: Prepare and practice responses to common interview questions, such as "Tell me about yourself" or "What are your strengths and weaknesses?" Consider recording yourself or practicing with a friend to improve your delivery and confidence.

- Be familiar with the technology used in the interview process: Understand the technology used in the interview, such as the video conferencing tool or chatbot interface, and test it beforehand to ensure it's working properly.

- Ensure your internet connection and computer equipment are reliable: Make sure your internet connection and computer equipment, such as your webcam and microphone, are reliable and functioning well. Consider using headphones or a headset to ensure good sound quality.

Tips for Success in AI-Enabled Job Interviews:

- Speak clearly and concisely: Speak clearly and concisely to help the AI technology understand your responses. Avoid using filler words or overly complex language.

- Be aware of your body language and facial expressions: Being mindful of your body language and facial expressions, even in a remote interview setting, is crucial. Make sure you are visible to the camera and avoid slouching or fidgeting.

- Use simple and direct language: Use simple and direct language to help the AI technology understand your responses. Avoid using slang, technical jargon, or acronyms unless necessary.

- Provide concrete examples of your skills and experience: Provide specific and concrete examples of your skills and experience to demonstrate your suitability for the job. Use the STAR method (Situation, Task, Action, Result) to structure your responses.

- Ask relevant questions to show your interest and knowledge about the company and job position: Ask relevant questions to show your interest and knowledge about the company and job position. This can help demonstrate your engagement and curiosity about the role.

Potential Challenges in AI-Enabled Job Interviews:

- Technical difficulties: The technology used for the interview may not function properly, resulting in lost time, disrupted communication, or even the need to reschedule the interview.

- Lack of personal touch: Some applicants may feel uncomfortable with a virtual interview, as they do not have the opportunity to meet the interviewer face-to-face, shake their hand, or read their body language in person.

- Unfamiliarity with the technology: Applicants who are not comfortable with the technology used for the interview may become distracted or stressed, which could negatively affect their performance.

- Bias in algorithms: AI systems are designed by humans and may contain biases that could impact the hiring process. For example, an AI system could be programmed to favor candidates who share certain demographic characteristics, leading to discriminatory outcomes.

Ethics and Transparency in AI-Enabled Job Interviews:

- The importance of fairness and unbiasedness in AI algorithms

- How to identify and address bias or discrimination in AI algorithms

- The role of transparency and accountability in AI-enabled job interviews

- The responsibility of companies to ensure ethical and fair use of AI technology in the hiring process

Conclusion

It is essential for applicants to be aware of these potential challenges and to prepare accordingly. By familiarizing yourself with the technology, practicing your responses to common interview questions, and staying up to date on the latest trends in AI, you can increase your chances of success in an AI-enabled job interview.

CHAPTER 6: UPGRADING YOUR SKILLS FOR THE AGE OF AI: TRAINING AND EDUCATION

In today's job market, it's no secret that artificial intelligence (AI) is rapidly transforming the way we work. Jobs that were once done by humans are now being replaced by machines, and new jobs are emerging that require a different set of skills. To stay competitive in this rapidly evolving job market, it's essential to upgrade your skills and acquire new ones. In this chapter, we will explore the importance of training and education in the age of AI and provide tips on how to develop the skills that employers are looking for.

The Importance of Training and Education

- As technology continues to advance, the skills required to succeed in the job market are changing rapidly. Jobs that were once in high demand are becoming obsolete, and new jobs are emerging that require different skills. To remain competitive, it is essential to invest in training and education that will help you acquire the skills that employers are looking for. This may involve obtaining a degree or certification in a specific field or taking online courses to develop new skills.

Identifying In-Demand Skills

- To upgrade your skills for the age of AI, it's important to identify the skills that are currently in demand. Some of the most sought-after skills in the age of AI include data analysis, programming, machine learning, and cybersecurity. By focusing on developing these skills, you can increase your chances of landing a job in a high-growth field and staying ahead of the curve.

Online Learning Platforms

- There are many online learning platforms available that offer courses in a variety of fields. Platforms like Coursera, Udemy, and LinkedIn Learning offer courses in programming, data analysis, and other in-demand skills. These courses are typically self-paced, allowing you to learn at your own speed and on your own schedule.

Professional Certifications

- Professional certifications are a great way to demonstrate your expertise in a particular field. Certifications like Certified Information Systems Security Professional (CISSP) or the Amazon Web Services (AWS) Certified Solutions Architect are highly valued in the IT industry. These certifications can help you stand out from the competition and increase your chances of landing a job in a high-demand field.

Soft Skills

- In addition to technical skills, it's also important to develop soft skills like communication, critical thinking, and problem-solving. These skills are highly valued by employers and can set you apart from other candidates. To develop these skills, consider taking courses in public speaking, leadership, or project management.

Conclusion

Training and education are essential for anyone looking to upgrade their skills for the age of AI. By identifying in-demand skills, taking advantage of online learning platforms, obtaining professional certifications, and developing soft skills, you can position yourself as a valuable asset to any employer. As the job market continues to evolve, it's important to stay ahead of the curve and invest in your future by upgrading your skills and acquiring new ones.

CHAPTER 7: JOB OPPORTUNITIES IN EMERGING AI FIELDS

Artificial intelligence (AI) is one of the fastest-growing fields in technology, with new developments and applications emerging all the time. As the capabilities of AI continue to evolve, new opportunities are arising for individuals looking to break into the field. In this chapter, we'll explore some of the most promising emerging AI fields and the job opportunities they offer.

Natural Language Processing (NLP)

NLP is a branch of AI that focuses on teaching computers to understand and interpret human language. This technology has wide-ranging applications, from chatbots and virtual assistants to sentiment analysis and speech recognition. Some of the job opportunities in NLP include:

- NLP engineer: responsible for designing and building NLP systems that can analyze and understand human language.
- Data scientist: works on building and implementing machine learning models for NLP systems.
- Computational linguist: focuses on the science of language, developing algorithms and models that can be used to analyze and interpret natural language.

Autonomous Vehicles

Self-driving cars are one of the most exciting and rapidly developing areas of AI. These vehicles use a combination of sensors, cameras, and advanced algorithms to navigate roads and make decisions. The job opportunities in autonomous vehicles include:

- Software engineer: responsible for designing and developing the software that controls the vehicle's operations and decision-making.

- Sensor engineer: works on developing the sensors and cameras that allow the vehicle to "see" and interact with its environment.

- Machine learning engineer: develops and trains machine learning models that allow the vehicle to make complex decisions and react to changing conditions.

Healthcare

AI has the potential to revolutionize the healthcare industry, from improving patient outcomes to reducing costs. Some of the job opportunities in healthcare include:

- Medical data analyst: responsible for analyzing and interpreting medical data to identify trends and patterns that can improve patient care.

- Medical imaging specialist: uses machine learning and image processing algorithms to analyze medical images and identify potential health issues.

- Health informatics specialist: focuses on using technology to improve the efficiency and effectiveness of healthcare delivery.

Robotics

Robots are becoming increasingly sophisticated and versatile, thanks in part to AI. Some of the job opportunities in robotics include:

- Robotics engineer: responsible for designing and building robots with advanced AI capabilities.

- Control systems engineer: works on developing the algorithms and software that allow robots to move and interact with their environment.

- Robotics technician: responsible for testing and maintaining robots in a variety of settings, from manufacturing to healthcare.

Conclusion

AI is opening up a world of new job opportunities in a variety of emerging fields. Whether you're interested in NLP, autonomous vehicles, healthcare, or robotics, there are plenty of exciting and rewarding job opportunities to explore. By developing the skills and expertise needed in these fields, you can position yourself for a successful and fulfilling career in the age of AI.

CHAPTER 8: OVERCOMING THE CHALLENGES OF WORKING WITH AI AND ROBOTS

As artificial intelligence (AI) and robotics continue to advance, more and more jobs are being impacted. While these technologies have the potential to improve productivity, they also present a range of challenges that can be difficult to overcome. In this chapter, we'll explore the challenges of working with AI and robots and provide strategies for addressing them.

Challenges of Working with AI and Robots

1. Fear of job loss: The most common challenge associated with AI and robotics is the fear of job loss. As machines become more capable of performing tasks that were previously done by humans, many workers are worried that their jobs will be eliminated. This fear can be particularly acute in industries that are heavily reliant on automation, such as manufacturing.
2. Complexity of technology: Another challenge of working with AI and robots is the complexity of the technology. These systems are often highly advanced and require specialized knowledge and expertise to operate. This can be intimidating for workers who are not familiar with the technology and can make it difficult for them to adapt to new work environments.
3. Lack of training: In many cases, workers are not adequately trained to work with AI and robots. This

can lead to a range of problems, including reduced productivity and safety concerns. Without proper training, workers may not understand how to operate the technology or may not be aware of the potential risks associated with its use.
4. Ethical concerns: As AI and robotics become more advanced, there are increasing concerns about their impact on society. For example, there are concerns that these technologies could be used to automate jobs that require human judgment and decision-making, such as those in the legal or medical fields. Additionally, there are concerns about the potential for bias and discrimination in AI systems.

Strategies for Overcoming the Challenges

1. Upskilling and reskilling: One of the most effective strategies for overcoming the challenges of working with AI and robots is to invest in upskilling and reskilling. By developing new skills and knowledge, workers can increase their value to employers and reduce the risk of job loss. This can involve taking courses or training programs in areas such as data analysis, programming, or robotics.
2. Collaboration: Collaboration between humans and machines can be a powerful way to improve productivity and reduce the risk of job loss. For example, machines can be used to perform routine, repetitive tasks, while humans can focus on more complex and creative work. This can result in a more productive and fulfilling work environment.
3. Training and education: Providing workers with adequate training and education is essential for ensuring their safety and productivity when working with AI and robots. This can involve providing hands-on

training and safety procedures, as well as education on the ethical and social implications of these technologies.
4. Ethical considerations: Addressing the ethical considerations of AI and robotics is essential for ensuring their responsible use. This can involve implementing ethical frameworks and guidelines, ensuring that AI systems are transparent and explainable, and addressing the potential for bias and discrimination.

Conclusion

Working with AI and robots presents a range of challenges, from the fear of job loss to ethical concerns. However, by investing in upskilling and reskilling, collaborating with machines, providing adequate training and education, and addressing ethical considerations, workers can successfully navigate this new landscape and thrive in the age of automation.

CHAPTER 9: BALANCING THE HUMAN TOUCH AND AI IN YOUR CAREER

As AI continues to play an increasingly important role in the workplace, many workers are concerned about how it will affect their jobs. While AI can improve efficiency and accuracy in certain tasks, it is important to maintain a balance between the human touch and AI to ensure that the needs of both the employer and employees are met. In this chapter, we will explore how to achieve this balance and provide tips for maximizing the benefits of both human and AI contributions to your career.

The Importance of the Human Touch

One of the main reasons that the human touch is so important in the workplace is that humans bring a unique set of skills and abilities to the table that cannot be replicated by machines. For example, humans have the ability to think creatively, make judgments based on context, and provide empathy and emotional support. These skills are essential in many industries, including healthcare, education, and the arts, where human interaction is key.

The Benefits of AI

While the human touch is important, there are many benefits to using AI in the workplace. AI can automate repetitive and time-consuming tasks, freeing up humans to focus on more complex and valuable work. It can also provide insights and analytics that help humans make better decisions, and it can improve accuracy and efficiency in many areas of the workplace.

Finding the Right Balance

The key to balancing the human touch and AI in your career is to understand the strengths and limitations of each. AI is best suited for tasks that are repetitive, data-driven, and rule-based. Humans, on the other hand, excel at tasks that require creativity, critical thinking, and emotional intelligence.

One approach to finding the right balance is to use AI as a tool to support and augment human work, rather than replacing it altogether. For example, in healthcare, AI can assist doctors in diagnosing diseases by analyzing patient data and providing recommendations. However, it cannot replace the human touch that is necessary for providing compassionate care and emotional support to patients.

Another approach is to use AI to enhance human capabilities, rather than replace them. For example, AI can provide real-time translation for people who speak different languages, allowing them to communicate more effectively. This can help to bridge cultural and language barriers and enable people to work together more effectively.

Ultimately, finding the right balance between the human touch and AI in your career requires careful consideration of the strengths and limitations of each. By understanding the unique skills and capabilities of humans and the benefits of AI, you can find ways to use technology to enhance human work, rather than replace it. This approach can lead to more efficient, effective, and fulfilling work experiences that benefit both employees and employers.

CHAPTER 10: STAYING AHEAD OF THE CURVE: FUTURE-PROOFING YOUR CAREER IN THE AGE OF AI

In today's rapidly evolving job market, staying ahead of the curve is essential for career success. As artificial intelligence (AI) and automation continue to transform the job market, it's important to future-proof your career by developing skills that are in high demand and embracing new technologies. In this chapter, we will explore strategies for future-proofing your career in the age of AI.

Stay Up-to-Date with Emerging Technologies

To stay ahead of the curve, it's important to stay up-to-date with emerging technologies. This includes not only AI but also related technologies like blockchain, the Internet of Things (IoT), and cloud computing. Keep an eye on emerging trends and try to identify how they might impact your industry. Attend industry conferences and read industry publications to stay informed about the latest developments.

Develop a Growth Mindset

To future-proof your career, it's important to develop a growth mindset. This means being open to learning new things, taking on new challenges, and embracing change. Instead of fearing change, see it as an opportunity to grow and develop new skills. Be willing to take risks and try new things.

Build a Strong Professional Network

Building a strong professional network is essential for staying ahead of the curve in your career. Connect with industry experts and thought leaders in your field, attend networking events, and join professional organizations. This will help you stay informed about the latest trends and developments in your industry and provide opportunities for learning and growth.

Develop Transferable Skills

As the job market evolves, it's important to develop transferable skills that can be applied in a variety of industries. These might include skills like communication, critical thinking, and problem-solving. By developing these skills, you can position yourself as a valuable asset in any industry.

Embrace Lifelong Learning

In the age of AI, lifelong learning is more important than ever. This means taking advantage of opportunities to learn and grow throughout your career. This might include taking courses, attending workshops, or pursuing certifications. By embracing lifelong learning, you can stay ahead of the curve and future-proof your career.

Be Agile and Adaptable

To future-proof your career in the age of AI, it's important to be agile and adaptable. This means being able to pivot quickly when the job market changes and being open to taking on new roles and responsibilities. Be willing to adapt to new technologies and new ways of working.

Conclusion

Future-proofing your career in the age of AI is essential for career success. By staying up-to-date with emerging technologies, developing a growth mindset, building a strong professional network, developing transferable skills, embracing lifelong learning, and being agile and adaptable, you can position yourself for success in a rapidly evolving job market. Remember to be proactive in managing your career and stay ahead of the curve by being open to change and taking advantage of new opportunities for learning and growth.

CHAPTER 11: ETHICAL CONSIDERATIONS FOR AI-ENABLED CAREERS: MAKING RESPONSIBLE CHOICES

As AI becomes more prevalent in the workplace, it is important to consider the ethical implications of its use. The use of AI can have both positive and negative impacts on the workplace, so it is important for professionals to take a thoughtful and responsible approach to its use.

The benefits of AI are numerous, including increased efficiency, accuracy, and productivity. However, there are also potential downsides, such as bias, job displacement, and loss of privacy. It is important for professionals to be aware of these issues and to make informed decisions about how AI is used in their workplace.

Here are 5 key ethical considerations for professionals working in AI-enabled careers:

1. *Bias in AI*

AI systems are only as unbiased as the data they are trained on. If the data used to train an AI system is biased, the system will be biased as well. This can have serious consequences, such as discrimination in hiring and lending decisions. It is important for professionals to be aware of this and to take steps to minimize bias in AI systems, such as using diverse data sets and regularly monitoring and auditing the system for bias.

2. Job displacement

The increased use of AI in the workplace has the potential to displace workers, particularly those in low-skilled jobs. It is important for professionals to consider the impact that their use of AI may have on the workforce and to take steps to minimize negative impacts. This may include retraining programs or other forms of support for workers whose jobs may be at risk.

3. Privacy concerns

The use of AI can raise significant privacy concerns, particularly when it comes to the collection and use of personal data. Professionals should be aware of the data that is being collected and how it is being used, and should take steps to protect the privacy of individuals. This may include using data encryption, ensuring data is collected and used only for legitimate purposes, and allowing individuals to access, correct, and delete their personal data.

4. Transparency

It is important for professionals to be transparent about the use of AI in their workplace. This includes communicating the ways in which AI is being used, the data that is being collected, and how that data is being used. This can help to build trust with stakeholders, including employees, customers, and the broader community.

5. Governance and regulation

As AI becomes more prevalent in the workplace, there is a growing need for governance and regulation. It is important for professionals to be aware of the laws and regulations that govern the use of AI in their industry and to ensure that they are in compliance. Additionally, professionals should be involved in discussions about the development of new regulations and standards for the use of AI.

Conclusion

The use of AI in the workplace has the potential to bring significant benefits, but it is important for professionals to take a responsible and ethical approach to its use. By considering the potential impacts of AI and taking steps to minimize negative impacts, professionals can ensure that AI is used in a way that is beneficial to both the organization and society as a whole.

CHAPTER 12: WORKING WITH AI IN TEAMS: COLLABORATING WITH MACHINES AND HUMANS

As the use of artificial intelligence (AI) becomes more widespread in the workplace, the way we collaborate with machines and humans is changing. In order to work effectively with AI, it's important to understand the strengths and limitations of both humans and machines, and to find ways to collaborate in a way that maximizes each group's abilities. In this chapter, we will explore some of the key considerations for working with AI in teams, and provide tips for collaborating effectively with machines and humans.

Understanding the Strengths and Limitations of Humans and Machines

To work effectively with AI in teams, it's important to understand the strengths and limitations of both humans and machines. Humans are great at tasks that require creativity, critical thinking, and empathy, while machines are better suited for tasks that require speed, accuracy, and repetitive processing. By understanding these differences, teams can leverage the strengths of both humans and machines to work more efficiently and effectively.

Collaborating with Machines

When collaborating with machines, it's important to understand how they work and what they are capable of. Some tips for collaborating with machines include:

1. Provide clear instructions: Machines work best when they are given clear and specific instructions. When working with machines, it's important to provide detailed instructions to ensure that they can complete their tasks accurately.
2. Monitor performance: Machines can sometimes make errors, so it's important to monitor their performance to ensure that they are working as expected. Regular performance checks can help identify any issues early on and prevent larger problems down the line.
3. Continuously learn and adapt: AI is constantly evolving, and teams need to stay up to date with the latest developments to effectively collaborate with machines. This may involve attending training sessions or reading up on the latest research.

Collaborating with Humans

When collaborating with humans, it's important to foster an environment of open communication and collaboration. Some tips for collaborating with humans include:

1. Encourage open communication: Effective collaboration requires open communication, so it's important to create an environment where team members feel comfortable sharing their thoughts and ideas.
2. Embrace diversity: Teams with diverse backgrounds and skillsets are often more effective at problem-solving and generating new ideas. Embrace diversity and encourage team members to share their unique perspectives.
3. Be flexible: Teams need to be flexible and adaptable to respond to changing circumstances. Encourage team members to be open to change and to take on new challenges.

Maximizing Collaboration with AI

To maximize collaboration with AI, it's important to find ways to integrate machines into the team in a way that complements human abilities. Some tips for maximizing collaboration with AI include:

1. Set clear goals and objectives: To effectively collaborate with AI, teams need to have clear goals and objectives. This helps ensure that everyone is working towards a common goal.
2. Use AI to automate repetitive tasks: AI is well-suited for tasks that are repetitive and time-consuming. By automating these tasks, team members can focus on more creative and high-value tasks.
3. Use AI to generate insights: AI can be used to analyze large datasets and generate insights that may not be immediately obvious to humans. Teams can use these insights to make better decisions and identify new opportunities.

Conclusion

Working with AI in teams requires an understanding of the strengths and limitations of both humans and machines, and a willingness to collaborate in a way that maximizes each group's abilities. By fostering open communication, embracing diversity, and finding ways to integrate machines into the team, teams can work more effectively and achieve better outcomes.

CHAPTER 13: BUILDING YOUR PERSONAL BRAND IN THE DIGITAL AGE: STRATEGIES AND BEST PRACTICES

Building your personal brand is a critical aspect of establishing your online presence and reputation. To make a lasting impression on potential employers, clients, or customers, it's essential to invest time and effort in creating a personal brand that reflects your values, strengths, and unique qualities. In this chapter, we'll explore some effective strategies and best practices for building your personal brand in the digital age.

What is a Personal Brand?

Your personal brand is the image and reputation you cultivate for yourself, both online and offline. It is the way you present yourself to the world and the message you convey to your target audience. Your personal brand is what sets you apart from others and helps you stand out in a crowded marketplace.

Why is Personal Branding Important?

Personal branding is crucial in today's digital age, where a strong online presence is essential for professional success. Employers, clients, and customers are increasingly using social media and other online platforms to research potential candidates or business partners. Having a strong personal brand can help you establish credibility and differentiate yourself from others in your field.

Strategies For Building Your Personal Brand:

Define Your Unique Selling Proposition (USP)

Your USP is what sets you apart from others in your industry. To create an effective personal brand, it's essential to identify your strengths, skills, and unique qualities. Ask yourself what makes you different from others in your field and what value you can bring to your target audience.

Develop a Consistent Online Presence

To build a strong personal brand, it's important to develop a consistent online presence across all relevant platforms, such as LinkedIn, Twitter, and Instagram. Use a professional headshot and a consistent tone of voice in your bio and posts. Share content that reflects your expertise and interests, and engage with your followers and other influencers in your field.

Create Compelling Content

One of the best ways to establish yourself as an authority in your field is to create and share high-quality content that showcases your expertise. This can include blog posts, videos, podcasts, or social media updates. Focus on creating content that provides value to your target audience and positions you as a thought leader in your industry.

Network with Other Professionals

Building relationships with other professionals in your field can be a powerful way to establish your personal brand. Attend industry events and conferences, connect with other professionals on LinkedIn, and join online communities and forums related to your field. By sharing your knowledge and expertise and engaging with others, you can build a network of like-minded individuals who can support and promote your personal brand.

Best Practices For Personal Branding

Be Authentic and Transparent

A successful personal brand is based on authenticity and transparency. Be true to yourself and your values, and avoid the temptation to misrepresent yourself or your accomplishments. Share your experiences and insights in an open and honest way, and be responsive to feedback from your followers and peers.

Focus on Quality Over Quantity

When building your personal brand, it's important to focus on quality over quantity. Rather than trying to be everywhere at once, focus on creating high-quality content and establishing a strong presence on a few key platforms. This will help you build a more engaged and loyal following and avoid spreading yourself too thin.

Stay Up to Date on Industry Trends

To maintain your credibility and relevance as an expert in your field, it's essential to stay up to date on industry trends and developments. Follow industry blogs, attend conferences and webinars, and read industry publications to stay informed on the latest news and best practices in your field.

Be Consistent and Persistent

Consistency and persistence are key to building a strong

personal brand in the digital age. To be consistent, you need to develop a clear and distinct brand message that you consistently communicate across all your online and offline channels. This message should be aligned with your values, goals, and unique selling proposition.

One of the best ways to stay consistent is to create a style guide for your brand. A style guide is a document that outlines the visual and messaging elements of your brand, including the colors, fonts, logos, taglines, and tone of voice. This helps ensure that all your communications are consistent and aligned with your brand.

Persistence is also important. Building a strong personal brand takes time and effort, and it's essential to stay persistent and committed to your brand message. Consistently creating and sharing valuable content, engaging with your audience, and attending networking events can help you build a strong and recognizable brand over time.

It's important to remember that building a personal brand is a continuous process, and you need to stay committed and consistent to achieve success. Don't be afraid to experiment, try new things, and adjust your approach based on what works and what doesn't. Stay open to feedback, be willing to learn and grow, and most importantly, be true to yourself and your values.

CHAPTER 14: OVERCOMING AGEISM AND BIAS IN THE AI-DRIVEN JOB MARKET

As artificial intelligence (AI) continues to transform the job market, it's important to acknowledge that it can also contribute to ageism and bias. AI can be programmed with implicit biases, which can affect its decision-making and lead to discrimination against certain groups. Additionally, older workers may face age discrimination when it comes to hiring and promotions, as younger workers are often perceived as being more tech-savvy and adaptable to the latest technologies.

In order to overcome ageism and bias in the AI-driven job market, there are several strategies that job seekers can employ:

Stay up to date with the latest technologies

One way to counter the perception that older workers are less tech-savvy is to stay up-to-date with the latest technology. Attend training sessions and conferences, and familiarize yourself with the latest software and tools. This will not only help you to perform your job better, but it will also demonstrate to employers that you are adaptable and eager to learn.

Focus on your skills and experience

When applying for jobs, focus on your skills and experience, rather than your age. Highlight your accomplishments and the value that you can bring to the organization. Emphasize your experience in the industry and your ability to collaborate effectively with other team members.

Consider taking courses in AI

To improve your job prospects in the age of AI, consider taking courses in AI and related fields. This will demonstrate to employers that you are familiar with the latest technology and that you are committed to staying up-to-date in your field. There are many online courses available, and some institutions even offer certificates and degrees in AI.

Be aware of the biases in AI

To combat bias in the AI-driven job market, it's important to be aware of biases in AI systems. These biases can affect everything from resume screening to hiring decisions, and can perpetuate existing inequalities in the job market. As a job seeker, you can research the AI systems that organizations use and make sure that they are not contributing to bias and discrimination.

Network with others in your industry

Networking is an important strategy for job seekers of any age, but it can be especially important for older workers who may face ageism in the job market. Attend industry events and join professional organizations to connect with others in your field. This can help you to learn about job opportunities and build relationships with potential employers.

Conclusion

Ageism and bias can be significant challenges in the AI-driven job market. However, there are strategies that job seekers can use to overcome these challenges, including staying up-to-date with the latest technology, focusing on their skills and experience, taking courses in AI and related fields, being aware of biases in AI, and networking with others in their industry. By employing these strategies, job seekers can position themselves for success in the age of AI.

CHAPTER 15: THE FUTURE OF WORK: ANTICIPATING AND ADAPTING TO AI-DRIVEN CHANGES

As the use of artificial intelligence (AI) becomes more widespread, it is changing the nature of work in many industries. In the years ahead, the continued evolution of AI will bring about significant changes in the job market. In this chapter, we will explore what these changes are likely to be and how individuals can adapt to them to prepare for the future of work.

The Changing Landscape of Work

The rapid development of AI is transforming the way we work. In many industries, automation is already replacing some jobs, while creating new ones that require a different set of skills. In the years ahead, these trends are likely to accelerate, creating both opportunities and challenges for workers.

Some jobs are at a higher risk of being automated than others. Jobs that are routine and involve repetitive tasks are most likely to be automated. However, jobs that require creativity, critical thinking, and interpersonal skills are less likely to be automated. This means that workers who can adapt to these changes and develop new skills will be better positioned to thrive in the future.

Preparing for the Future of Work

To prepare for the future of work, individuals must take a proactive approach to their careers. This means developing new skills, staying up-to-date with technological advancements, and embracing change.

One way to prepare for the future of work is to focus on developing skills that are less likely to be automated. This includes skills like problem-solving, critical thinking, creativity, and interpersonal communication. These skills are highly valued by employers and are less likely to be replaced by machines.

Another way to prepare for the future of work is to stay up-to-date with technological advancements. This means learning about the latest AI technologies and how they are being used in various industries. By staying informed, individuals can identify new opportunities and better position themselves for success.

Adapting to the Future of Work

As the nature of work changes, individuals must be prepared to adapt to new roles and responsibilities. This may mean developing new skills or learning to work with AI technologies.
One way to adapt to the future of work is to be open to new roles and opportunities. This means being willing to take on new challenges and responsibilities, even if they are outside of your comfort zone. It also means being open to new industries and sectors, as many emerging industries may offer new opportunities for growth and development.

Another way to adapt to the future of work is to learn to work with AI technologies. This means understanding how AI works and how it can be used to enhance work processes. It also means being able to work with machines in a collaborative manner, using AI to augment human capabilities.

5 Key Takeaways:

1. Skills that will be in demand: As AI becomes more prevalent in the workplace, certain skills will be in high demand. These may include programming, data analysis, cybersecurity, and machine learning. Workers who possess these skills will likely have an advantage over those who don't, as companies will need professionals who can develop and maintain AI systems.
2. The impact on job opportunities: As AI becomes more advanced, some jobs may become obsolete while new ones emerge. For example, automated systems may replace certain manual labor jobs, but new jobs may be created to design, build, and maintain those systems. Workers will need to be prepared to adapt to these changes, potentially by upgrading their skills or exploring new career paths.
3. The role of education: Education and training will play a key role in preparing workers for the changes brought about by AI. Schools and training programs will need to adapt their curricula to ensure that students are learning the skills that will be in demand in the job market. Continuing education programs may also become more important for workers who need to keep their skills up to date.
4. The importance of soft skills: While technical skills will be important, soft skills will also play a critical role in the future of work. For example, workers who possess strong communication and collaboration skills will be able to work more effectively in teams that include both humans and machines. Employers will also value workers who are adaptable, curious, and willing to learn.
5. The role of government and policy: As AI-driven changes impact the workforce, governments and policymakers will need to address issues related to employment, education, and training. This may include creating new programs to support workers who are displaced

by automation, promoting education and training programs that teach in-demand skills, and regulating the use of AI to ensure that it is used ethically and fairly.

Conclusion

The continued evolution of AI will bring about significant changes in the job market. Jobs that were once in high demand may become obsolete, while new jobs that require a different set of skills will emerge. To prepare for the future of work, individuals must take a proactive approach to their careers, developing new skills, staying up-to-date with technological advancements, and adapting to new roles and responsibilities. By doing so, individuals can position themselves for success in the age of AI.

CHAPTER 16: THE ROLE OF EMOTIONAL INTELLIGENCE IN THE AGE OF AI

As technology continues to advance, the rise of artificial intelligence (AI) is having a profound impact on the way we live and work. With the increasing use of AI and automation, the ability to connect with others and understand their emotions is becoming more important than ever. In this chapter, we'll explore the importance of emotional intelligence in the age of AI and how it can be developed to thrive in a world where machines are becoming more prevalent.

What is Emotional Intelligence?

Emotional intelligence (EI) is the ability to recognize, understand, and manage our own emotions, as well as the emotions of others. It involves skills such as empathy, self-awareness, self-regulation, and social skills, which are essential for building strong relationships and effective communication.

Why is Emotional Intelligence Important in the Age of AI?

With the increasing use of AI and automation, it is becoming more important than ever to have emotional intelligence skills. While machines are excellent at processing large amounts of data and making decisions based on that data, they lack the ability to recognize and respond to emotions in the way that humans can. This means that tasks requiring emotional intelligence skills, such as building relationships with clients, leading teams, and providing customer service, are likely to become more important in the future.

Developing Emotional Intelligence in the Age of AI

The good news is that emotional intelligence can be developed, even in the age of AI.

Here Are 5 Key Strategies For Building Emotional Intelligence Skills:

1. Practice Mindfulness: Mindfulness is the practice of being present in the moment and aware of our thoughts and feelings. By practicing mindfulness, we can increase our self-awareness and develop greater control over our emotions.
2. Focus on Empathy: Empathy is the ability to understand and share the feelings of others. By focusing on empathy, we can develop better communication skills, build stronger relationships, and provide better customer service.
3. Develop Social Skills: Social skills involve the ability to interact effectively with others. By developing social skills, we can improve our ability to work in teams, lead others, and collaborate effectively.
4. Seek Feedback: Seeking feedback from others can help us understand how our emotions and behaviors impact those around us. By being open to feedback, we can develop greater self-awareness and make changes to improve our emotional intelligence skills.
5. Practice Emotional Regulation: Emotional regulation involves the ability to manage our own emotions, even in challenging situations. By practicing emotional

regulation, we can maintain our composure, build resilience, and avoid overreacting in stressful situations.

Conclusion

As AI and automation continue to transform the workplace, emotional intelligence skills are becoming more important than ever. By developing emotional intelligence skills, individuals can build stronger relationships, communicate more effectively, and provide better customer service. While machines are excellent at processing data, they lack the ability to recognize and respond to emotions in the way that humans can. By combining the power of AI with emotional intelligence skills, we can create a more productive and fulfilling work environment.

CHAPTER 17: AI AND THE GIG ECONOMY: OPPORTUNITIES AND CHALLENGES

The gig economy is a rapidly growing sector of the job market, characterized by short-term contracts and freelance work. With the rise of Artificial Intelligence (AI), the gig economy is being transformed in ways that were previously unimaginable. In this chapter, we will explore the opportunities and challenges presented by AI in the gig economy.

Opportunities

1. Increased Efficiency: AI can help gig workers be more productive and efficient. By automating repetitive and time-consuming tasks, workers can focus on higher value activities that require creativity and innovation.
2. Expanded Customer Base: AI can help gig workers reach a wider customer base. With the use of chatbots and virtual assistants, businesses can provide 24/7 customer support to clients, regardless of their location. This can help gig workers expand their services beyond their local area.
3. Flexible Work Arrangements: AI can enable gig workers to work on their own terms. By automating routine tasks, gig workers have more control over their schedules, allowing them to work when they want and where they want.
4. Improved Quality of Work: AI can help gig workers deliver higher quality work by providing real-time

feedback and suggestions. AI-powered tools can help workers identify and correct errors, ensuring that their work meets the highest standards.

Challenges

1. Job Displacement: The biggest challenge of AI in the gig economy is job displacement. As AI becomes more sophisticated, some of the tasks that were previously performed by gig workers will be automated, leading to a reduction in demand for their services.
2. Skill Gaps: As AI transforms the nature of work, gig workers will need to acquire new skills to remain relevant. This can be challenging for those who are not tech-savvy or who lack access to training and educational opportunities.
3. Data Privacy and Security: With the increasing use of AI in the gig economy, data privacy and security are becoming major concerns. Gig workers need to be aware of the risks associated with sharing their personal and professional data with third-party platforms and ensure that they are taking appropriate measures to protect their information.
4. Fair Compensation: Gig workers may find it difficult to negotiate fair compensation for their work in the age of AI. As AI becomes more prevalent, the value of certain services may decrease, leading to a decline in wages for gig workers.

Conclusion

The gig economy is being transformed by the rise of AI, bringing both opportunities and challenges for gig workers. As AI becomes more prevalent, it is important for gig workers to stay up-to-date with the latest technological developments and acquire the skills needed to remain competitive. They should also be aware of the potential risks associated with the use of AI in the gig economy and take appropriate measures to protect themselves. Ultimately, the successful integration of AI into the gig economy will depend on the ability of gig workers and businesses to adapt to the changing nature of work.

CHAPTER 18: NAVIGATING THE GLOBAL JOB MARKET WITH AI: TIPS AND STRATEGIES

The world is increasingly becoming more interconnected, and as a result, many organizations are looking to hire top talent from across the globe. The use of AI in the recruitment process has made it easier for organizations to find and hire the right candidates. However, for job seekers, navigating the global job market can be challenging, especially when dealing with different cultures, time zones, and job requirements. In this chapter, we will provide some tips and strategies to help job seekers navigate the global job market with the help of AI.

Research the Job Market:

The first step in navigating the global job market is to research the job market. The internet is a great resource for job seekers looking for jobs overseas. Many job search engines provide job listings from around the world, and some even offer job alerts to notify you when new job openings are available. In addition, social media platforms like LinkedIn can be an excellent tool for connecting with recruiters and potential employers in other countries. AI-powered tools like chatbots and job matching algorithms can help you to find the best fit for your skills and experience.

Understand Cultural Differences:

One of the biggest challenges in the global job market is understanding and adapting to cultural differences. Before applying for jobs in a different country, it is important to research and learn about the cultural norms, values, and customs. This can help you to understand what is expected of you and how to behave in a professional setting. For instance, in some cultures, it is considered rude to talk about personal matters during an interview. AI-powered cultural intelligence tools can help you to understand different cultures and customs, and how they affect the workplace.

Learn New Skills:

The global job market is highly competitive, and employers are looking for candidates with a diverse skillset. To increase your chances of landing a job in a different country, it is important to learn new skills and stay up-to-date with the latest trends and technologies. Online learning platforms like Udemy and Coursera offer a wide range of courses in various fields, including AI and other emerging technologies. AI-powered learning platforms can personalize learning paths to your needs, interests, and career goals.

Network with Professionals:

Networking with professionals in your field is an excellent way to learn about job opportunities in other countries. Attend conferences, seminars, and workshops, and connect with professionals in your industry. Social media platforms like LinkedIn and Twitter can help you to connect with people from all over the world. AI-powered tools like social listening and recommendation engines can help you find relevant people and content, and suggest groups and communities to join.

Be Prepared for Interviews:

If you are applying for a job in a different country, you may be asked to participate in a virtual interview. It is important to prepare for these interviews by researching the company and the job, and practicing your responses to common interview questions. In addition, be aware of the time difference and make sure to schedule the interview at a time that is convenient for both you and the interviewer. AI-powered interview preparation tools can help you to practice and improve your interview skills.

Conclusion

Navigating the global job market with AI requires research, adaptability, and continuous learning. Job seekers need to be aware of cultural differences, learn new skills, network with professionals, and be prepared for virtual interviews. AI-powered tools can help job seekers to find the best job opportunities, learn new skills, and prepare for interviews. By following these tips and strategies, job seekers can increase their chances of success in the global job market.

CHAPTER 19: THE INTERSECTION OF AI AND CREATIVITY: OPPORTUNITIES AND CHALLENGES FOR CREATIVE CAREERS

The field of creative careers, which encompasses industries such as art, music, film, advertising, and design, is currently undergoing a transformation as artificial intelligence (AI) is becoming more prevalent in the creative process. While some may worry that AI could eventually replace human creativity, others see it as a valuable tool that can enhance and expand the creative process. In this chapter, we will explore the opportunities and challenges that the intersection of AI and creativity presents for individuals pursuing creative careers.

Opportunities

1. Increased Efficiency: One of the most significant advantages of using AI in creative fields is that it can increase the efficiency of the creative process. For example, AI can assist with tasks such as data analysis, research, and administrative tasks, freeing up more time for creatives to focus on the actual creative work.
2. New Possibilities: AI can enable creatives to explore new possibilities and push the boundaries of their work. For example, machine learning algorithms can analyze and identify patterns in large data sets, which can help creatives find inspiration and generate new ideas.

3. Collaboration: AI can also facilitate collaboration between humans and machines. For example, AI algorithms can analyze a creative project and provide suggestions or generate alternative designs that can inspire human creatives to explore new directions.
4. Personalization: AI can help creatives create more personalized and targeted work. For example, AI can analyze large data sets to help creatives better understand their audience and create work that resonates with them.

Challenges

1. Job Displacement: As AI becomes more prevalent in creative fields, some may worry that it could lead to job displacement. While it's true that some tasks previously done by humans may be automated, it's also likely that new jobs will be created in the field of AI, such as those focused on training, developing, and maintaining AI systems.
2. Privacy Concerns: AI relies on large amounts of data, and there is always a risk that this data could be misused. Creatives who use AI must be aware of privacy concerns and ensure that they are using the data ethically and responsibly.
3. Bias: AI algorithms are only as unbiased as the data they are trained on. This means that there is a risk of bias in AI-generated work. Creatives must be aware of this and work to ensure that their AI-generated work is inclusive and representative.
4. Overreliance: While AI can be a valuable tool in the creative process, there is a risk of overreliance on the technology. Creatives must remember that AI should be used to enhance their work, not replace it entirely.

Strategies for Creatives

1. Stay informed: Creatives must stay up-to-date on the latest advancements in AI and how they may impact their field. This will enable them to stay ahead of the curve and adapt to changes as they arise.
2. Embrace AI: Creatives should not view AI as a threat, but rather as a valuable tool that can enhance their work. Embracing AI can help creatives stay competitive and find new opportunities for growth.
3. Work with AI experts: To make the most of AI, creatives should collaborate with AI experts who can help them understand the technology and how it can be used in their work.
4. Be aware of ethical considerations: Creatives must be aware of the ethical considerations involved in using AI, including issues of bias, privacy, and overreliance on technology.

Conclusion

The intersection of AI and creativity is both exciting and challenging. While AI has already revolutionized many creative industries and will continue to do so, there are also concerns about its potential impact on human creativity and the ethical considerations surrounding AI-generated content. However, if we embrace the opportunities presented by AI and take an active role in shaping its development and use, we can harness its power to enhance, rather than replace, human creativity.

One of the key takeaways from this chapter is that AI is not a threat to human creativity, but rather a tool that can be used to augment it. AI can help creative professionals work more efficiently, generate new ideas and insights, and reach larger audiences. However, it is important to recognize that AI is not a substitute for human creativity and that creativity is an innately human trait that cannot be replicated by machines.

To ensure that AI is used responsibly in creative fields, it is important for industry professionals, policymakers, and researchers to work together to establish ethical guidelines and best practices for its development and use. This includes ensuring that AI-generated content is transparently labeled and giving credit to the humans who trained the algorithms. It also means fostering diversity and inclusion in the development of AI technologies to ensure that they are not biased or discriminatory.

As AI continues to evolve and impact the creative industries, it is important for professionals to stay up-to-date with the latest developments and be willing to adapt to new technologies and practices. By embracing AI and using it to enhance human creativity, we can create a future where both humans and machines work together to achieve even greater levels of innovation and artistic expression.

CHAPTER 20: AI AND YOUR PERSONAL LIFE: FINDING WORK-LIFE BALANCE IN THE DIGITAL AGE

In recent years, technology has dramatically changed the way we live our lives. In particular, the rise of artificial intelligence (AI) has brought many benefits and conveniences to our daily routines, but it has also brought new challenges to finding a balance between work and personal life. With the ever-increasing pace of technological change, it's important to understand how to integrate AI into our personal lives while still maintaining a healthy work-life balance.

The Benefits of AI in Personal Life

AI is revolutionizing the way we approach our personal lives, providing us with personalized recommendations, improving our time management, and making everyday tasks easier and more efficient. Here are a few ways in which AI can benefit our personal lives:

Personalized Recommendations

One of the most significant benefits of AI is its ability to analyze large amounts of data and provide us with personalized recommendations. Whether it's music, movies, books, or news articles, AI algorithms can learn our preferences and suggest content that we are likely to enjoy. This can save us a significant amount of time that we would otherwise spend searching for content on our own.

Time Management

AI can help us manage our time more efficiently. For example, virtual assistants like Siri or Alexa can help us schedule appointments, set reminders, and even create to-do lists. AI-powered apps like Trello and Asana can also help us manage our tasks more effectively, ensuring that we are staying on top of our work and personal obligations.

Simplifying Everyday Tasks

AI is also making everyday tasks more manageable. For example, with the rise of smart home technology, we can use voice commands to control our lights, thermostat, and even our kitchen appliances. Chatbots and virtual assistants can help us order groceries, make restaurant reservations, and even book travel.

Challenges to Work-Life Balance in the Digital Age

While AI provides many benefits to our personal lives, it can also pose challenges to work-life balance. Here are a few ways in which AI can make it more difficult to achieve work-life balance.

Constant Availability

With the rise of remote work and the ubiquity of smartphones, it can be challenging to disconnect from work. AI-powered tools can make it easier to work remotely, but they can also make it more difficult to disconnect from work and maintain a healthy work-life balance.

Information Overload

With the abundance of information available on the internet, it can be challenging to prioritize what is essential and what is not. AI algorithms can provide us with an endless stream of content, making it difficult to unplug and unwind.

Blurring of Work and Personal Boundaries

AI can also blur the lines between work and personal life. For example, using the same device for work and personal use can make it challenging to separate work and personal activities. Similarly, the constant availability of work-related communications can make it challenging to find time for personal activities.

Strategies for Achieving Work-Life Balance in the Age of AI

To maintain a healthy work-life balance in the digital age, it's essential to set boundaries and use technology to our advantage. Here are a few strategies for achieving work-life balance in the age of AI:

Set Boundaries

To maintain a healthy work-life balance, it's important to set clear boundaries between work and personal life. This means creating a separate workspace for work-related activities, scheduling specific work hours, and turning off notifications outside of work hours.

Use Technology to Your Advantage

While technology can pose challenges to work-life balance, it can also be used to our advantage. For example, virtual assistants can help us manage our schedules and tasks, freeing up more time for us to focus on other important aspects of our lives. We can also use technology to stay connected with loved ones, no matter where we are in the world. Video conferencing tools can help us have face-to-face conversations, even if we are miles apart. Additionally, many organizations now offer remote work options, which can provide more flexibility in our schedules and eliminate time spent commuting. By using technology in smart and strategic ways, we can strike a better balance between our personal and professional lives.

ABOUT THE AUTHOR

Michael R. Watson

Michael Richard Watson is a talent acquisition expert and artificial intelligence enthusiast who is dedicated to using cutting-edge technologies to revolutionize the world of work. Michael's passion for work began in his early life, as he grew up with military parents who instilled in him the values of hard work, dedication, and service to others. His father dropped out of high school at 16 to join the Navy, and his mother served in both the Air Force and Marines, so Michael knows firsthand the importance of having a strong work ethic and a sense of purpose.

After years of experience in corporate HR and talent acquisition for companies such as Aerotek, Robert Half, Polycom, Western Digital, Workday, Rambus, and Gigamon, Michael joined the artificial intelligence startup Eightfold.ai. As a former customer of Eightfold.ai, he has unique first-hand knowledge of how AI is being used to hire and retain talent. At Eightfold, Michael is part of a team that is using AI for good, mapping skills to opportunities and enabling the right career for everyone in the world. As the Head of Global Customer Evangelism for Eightfold's products and solutions, Michael frequently interacts with business leaders, customer executives and government officials to amplify the power of Eightfold's artificial intelligence (AI) and their vision to use artificial intelligence for good and enable the right career for everyone in the world. Michael believes that AI has the potential to help individuals find fulfilling and meaningful work, and he is dedicated to ensuring that everyone has access to the right career opportunities. He is passionate about helping individuals find work that aligns with their unique skills and interests, and he believes that AI can be a powerful tool to help people achieve their career goals.

Michael is a thought leader in the field of talent acquisition and artificial intelligence, and he is committed to using his expertise to help organizations and individuals navigate the rapidly changing world of work. He is a frequent speaker and writer on topics related to AI, talent acquisition, and career development, and he is always looking for new and innovative ways to use technology to improve people's lives.

Michael attended Fresno State University where he studied Criminology. When he is not working, Michael is busy working on his family's farm and dedicates a lot of time to coaching youth baseball and softball in his community. He is married and has two children.

www.ingramcontent.com/pod-product-compliance
Lightning Source LLC
Chambersburg PA
CBHW031539210526
45464CB00003B/1076